D.M. Langdon is also the author of

A Treatise on the Soul (2014),

Universal Wisdom for the Golden Age (2014),

Death Becomes You (2016),

Dream World (2017), and

A Girl Has No Age (2019).

A SAINT FOR ANY SEASON

D.M. LANGDON

Copyright © 2020 D.M. Langdon
Cover Art by Ruby D.L.

ISBN: 978-1-922409-23-2
Published by Vivid Publishing
A division of Fontaine Publishing Group
P.O. Box 948, Fremantle
Western Australia 6959
www.vividpublishing.com.au

A catalogue record for this
book is available from the
National Library of Australia

For my dear parents, John and Margaret

The recesses of time seek to gather all who play a part in life's rich pantomime. The Holy are gathered, they come again to spread God's Word, and Heaven knows their names. They arise like butterflies after the storm, their beauty there for all to savour. Fragile as the wind, they whisper in the truth to set love free.

Prologue

No-one ever sets out to become a Saint. Most Saints lived their life as we all do, day by day, taking the highs with the lows, surviving as best they could in a world much harsher than it is now. It is often many years or even centuries later that the powers of the day decide, in retrospection, that the lives of the humble Christian Saints were far from ordinary. Their lives reveal both the beauty and the terror of early Christianity.

This book allows you to follow in the footsteps of one of the early Christian Saints, just for a day or two, as he navigates the journey of his life. I'll let you work out who it might be, remembering, of course, that mankind's recorded history does not always have a monopoly on the truth in regard to its accuracy and completeness.

You will be delighted by the internal reflections of this Saint as he connects with the divine light of God. Was he successful in his holy mission? I'll let you, the reader, be the judge.

His messages are still relevant to this day, and many readers will see the correlations with our modern times. The altars at which we choose to worship may have varied, but the fundamental societal idols are much the same: mankind is still in thrall to the artificial edifices of materialism, power, and greed.

A Saint For Any Season will remind you of the full potential that exists within us all when we open our hearts and minds to the eternal wisdom of old. This truth will set us free from the pain and sorrow of the human condition.

May this be the season of triumph for your Soul.

D.M. Langdon

Chapter 1

Sustenance for our Souls.

⋯⋯

I sit on the wooden chair at my laden desk, the piles of manuscripts curling at the edges. The candlelight flickers. I am alone in the peace and harmony of the cell-like room, an ante room of sorts, which is my sanctuary. This room is my comfort, my retreat when not serving the masses the ministrations of the day.

My mind wanders. How old I must be now. I see my shadow projected on the wall, stooped, with neck hunched over. Clothed in an old robe and cape, I am a swaddled mass.

I offer a prayer to God Almighty, a gentle, personal offering of gratitude and welcome. I ask forgiveness for my Soul, for I understand that no man is perfect, even – especially, perhaps – a man of God. We are all a work in progress.

I ignore the growl of my stomach. When was it I last ate? The urge to write compels me. I sit down, quill in hand poised above the parchment. Where do I begin? What was that thought I just had? Ah, the wandering mind of old age, focussed more on the past than the present. So much to ponder. So much contemplation of life's great mysteries, with much time spent fossicking in the crammed and disorganised drawers of memory.

A word, a simple word, starts the process flowing. I am cocooned in a flood of love, peace, and contentment, as I lay my wisdom down. The words flow, they have a life of their own. They flow easily from my heart to my hand, the fluidity of the process always astounding, always comforting. It is the wisdom of the Ages, God's Word to share with all who wish to understand the righteous way to live. Wisdom for those who seek guidance and shelter from the harshness of their life – shelter in God's Word and the Kingdom of Heaven.

The chill creeps in. The stone floor is icy now and my legs are numb. The fire is fed, a small mercy in my advancing years. Arthritis is a cruel reminder of a man's mortality and the lost dawn of youth. The flames jump and flicker, crackling and hissing, offering an easing of the loneliness of solitude. Fire is mankind's solid companion in the absence of all else. Fire is comforting, entertaining, magical, until deadly. It is an equal friend and foe in the travails of mankind's survival.

The air warms and my lungs are comforted. Back to the task at hand, I connect with the higher vibration of the divine light. A softness envelops me as I continue with my task – the Doctrines. These documents are an ever-evolving continuation of the creeds started in earlier years with Paul, and they are still a mighty work in progress. I often get side-tracked, this I do readily admit, but such major works should not be rushed. They contain such important wisdom of the Ages, taking many moons to complete and perfect. But what is perfection? Mankind will never know perfection until they reach the Kingdom of God.

Nonetheless, mankind is perfect in its imperfection, you could say, as a creation of God the Almighty. But real perfection in our Earthly sphere eludes us all, no matter how righteousness rules our day. For our thoughts deceive us, and thoughts are the energy that surrounds and envelops us. Doubt, hate, spite, jealousy – there are many thoughts to keep at bay as we go about our lives. But progress we do.

Perseverance and dedication are the keys to our deliverance. I have dedicated my life to God, and to Jesus, and I am comforted in the knowledge that my life has been fruitful. Jesus has been my rock, my inspiration, ever since I first heard him speak so many years ago in the cave of light. Still I hunger so, and yet I have been fed. And I will continue to feed the blessed brethren with the wisdom of the Word. This, I understand, is my duty and my passion. It is my purpose of being.

I stand proud in the glory of the Word, and the understanding that the inspiration I receive is part of who I am. It is the task I agreed to in this life. For I am a true believer, and the joy I feel when communicating the Word is a joy that is indescribable; a joy to see me to the end of my days, old as I might be.

In truth, I am surprised I have lived this long – three score and ten and counting. My body is old and weak. Living with these aches and pains is a torturous existence, but my mind is focussed on the task at hand. There is still so much to record! And my destiny will become me, as it becomes all of us.

I know I am eternal. I know I am loved by God. Will I have time to finish my good works? Perhaps my next life will see a continuation of this role as a Scribe of God. I am never rid of the notion that there is still much to do, but so little time left. I do feel that time is against me now. I pray to God, to Father Time, to come to my rescue and allow me time to complete these major founding documents for the church. This will allow me such satisfaction and pride.

I pause to reflect on those I have outlived. They were my friends one and all, followers of Christ, and many succumbed to their own painful demise. Such a tragedy to unfold when there is so much wanton violence, wastefulness of life, and destruction of the human spirit.

Such martyrdom, what is it all for? I know I do not have all of the answers, some things are simply beyond my reach. Untold pain and sorrow; so many lessons for mankind. The agony of Christ, and the death of many followers – why were they all taken so soon? Such a destiny defies me. We still had so much to accomplish.

Was it all worth it? I ponder this question with anguish. Yes, of course! Are all the wise words and the healing miracles to be lost in obscurity, eventually consigned to the dust-pile of memory? Not so! Not if I continue to work hard transcribing the holy scriptures with meticulous diligence. I will deliver the Word of God and educate the truth-seekers, just as Jesus intended. They deserve nothing less. Wisdom comes to those who seek answers to the mysteries of life.

Become the Light and the Light becomes you –
enlightenment in all its glory!

The life of Jesus is the template we should follow. Love and light, generosity of spirit, and compassion to all – is it so hard for us to comprehend such simple, yet profound wisdom? Why do I feel I have to repeat his words ad nauseum? What is it about humanity that ensures that greed and self-interest reign supreme? What is the tipping point, I wonder?

I focus the mind and get back to work as my eyes begin to tire in the dim light. The flickering shadows are hypnotic and soothing. My hand is steady as I focus on the parchment once more. The purity of the words and the simplicity of the message, as usual, astounds me:

> *Faith is the bread of life. Faith is the sustenance*
> *of the masses; the beauty of the dawn as the sun*
> *rises once more.*

Our Soul is a mirror to the Lord. We must not reflect darkness, misery, and pain. Instead, reflect light and love, and good deeds to all. This is our purpose in life, to put our faith in God and trust that all is as it should be. The sun will continue to rise no matter the depth of darkness of night.

God has a plan for you, and acceptance of God in your life will open up the means to set you free from the tyranny of life. You will be freed from the horror that abounds in the schoolyard of life if you accept that you have 'free will' and your righteous choices and your good intentions are the keys to set you free from misery and despair.

Intend to be righteous in all that you do, and your spiritual pathway will open up before you. You will be tested always.

This is the flipside of faith and, indeed, of life, but you will know true purpose and your days will be fruitful. Righteousness of being is the simple recipe of life; such bounty for your Soul.

Life is of your making. Take joy in
all life offers. Understand that the fruit
on the vine of life is sweet and sour, and life
is in the choosing. Choose well, as your
choices will be with you in eternity.

I digress. How many times have I put this message forward? How many ways have I sought to demonstrate the truth? And yet, and yet... petty squabbles still abound. So many people – even from the church – still conspire to bring each other down. In plots that thicken in the night, the quest for power and glory seeks to rob them of their light. Power and greed rule the day; such gluttony to be sure.

Have they forgotten the simple words of Jesus? Have they forgotten our mission to bring the Kingdom of Heaven to Earth, to demonstrate love and compassion, feed the poor, heal the sick, and provide wisdom to the masses? All nourishment for the Soul. Is this goal out of touch to us now? I do despair it has come to this.

I have tried, Lord knows I have tried, but the pagans are gaining ground. The idolaters are pushing forward now, their superstitions growing with each new generation. Their quest for an easy life is supplicated by ever increasing rituals and sacrifices, principles of appeasement based on fear and favour, no less. Fear of life is their driving force. It drives the reason from their minds. Like children, they want immediate rewards. There is no patience for eternal salvation.

Oh, how I wish they could see what I see – the Heavenly Angels singing a chorus of love and joy to all those who bask in their glory. I am ready God, so ready, to leave this body behind. I am ready to go home. I am weary, and I am cold. Such coldness to the bone I cannot endure, but I trust in your divine plan for me, and I know there is still much work to be done. I persevere in the knowledge that I am purposeful, I am productive, and my faith is pure. I will not neglect my role as Scribe of the glorious Word.

Life is hard for most. Food is scarce, disease is plenty, and violence is in the air we breathe. Faith in God provides true purpose for the Soul. Faith provides an elevation to purity and grace, an upliftment from the drudgery and pain of life. Life is a test and progression is hard, yet we trudge along taking the knocks and disappointments in our stride. For what choice do we have? Do we hide away, drown our sorrows, and lash out at others when seeking a target to blame for our misfortunes?

Do we trust in God to salve our pain, or sacrifice what little we have to appease a pagan god? Which shall it be, ap-peasement or piety?

The heart knows the answer, even if the head
does not. The heart is willing, ever able, to heed
the call of Christ.

Immediate mollification of the masses is the growing trend now. A bonfire here, a circus there, a celebration of sorcery and sacrifice – what a truly frightening spectacle! No-one has the patience to spend their life banking on eternity. Eternal salvation is a lifetime away when drawn up against debauchery and cravenness. Riches of the soul cannot compete with riches of the pocket.

I am too old for this. I don't understand this wickedness upon them. I hide away, administering to the faithful. My church is my castle, my safety, and my fortress. I venture out less and less nowadays; my faithful servants run the errands of the day. The kindness of those who look after my physical needs is a blessing, to be sure.

I recognise the growling of my stomach again and realise I have not touched the platter of bread, cheese and grapes on my table, the chalice of wine warming now from the heat of the fire which fills the room. As I nibble, I muse that God's intention is clearly that we do not live on the Word alone. We must nurture and nourish the temple of our being, the house of our Spirit. Often, this is so hard to remember when I am pining for the spiritual, and the physical is just a tedious distraction. I eat away, impatient to fuel this old bag of bones and continue with my writing.

I feel the all too regular heaviness and empty my bladder into the chamber pot under the small, hard plank of the bed. It is so tedious to be bound to a physical existence, anchored to the moribundity of life. But God has created me thus, and so I acknowledge the blessing that I am. I vow to take better care of my physical vessel, the temple that houses my eternal Spirit, grotesque as it feels to me in my advancing years.

Oh, the vanity of youth! If only they realised what was to befall them, they would not waste a moment worrying about inconsequential issues of an immature mind. They would seize each day with both hands, climbing the mountains of their Souls to lay claim to the prosperity beyond, not while away their hours sleeping or plotting revenge for each slight, succumbing to the trivialities of life.

Many a time I said to you, the fruit grows on the vine. It ripens now and all will know the character of the wine.

Ah, to be young, with ego and insecurities running rampant, often in different directions! I do remember the boundless energy, the strength, the agility, the quickness of mind. Although I must admit I wasn't as physical as most. Sickly, perhaps, would best describe my constitution, however, I do recall the freshness of youth, awakening each day anew and raring to go. What a contrast to the infirmity of old age.

I always preferred to live an internal life. My physicality never interested me much. Most times I ignored it, to be truthful. I took it for granted, with just a vague awareness of walking through this physical world, and it was neither a hindrance, nor a help, to be attached to a mass of flesh. Increasingly though, as I aged, the awareness of the mismatch of mind and body dismayed me. My mind was lighter, increasingly elevated to the stars above, to the lighter and higher vibration of my Higher Self. Yet my body dragged heavily, grounded to Earth, seemingly decaying to a distant timepiece. Indeed, my body was held hostage to a different beat of my heart.

The flesh is a temptation and a joy of youthful endeavours. A body is to be enjoyed, with love, grace, and dignity, just as all of life is to be savoured and not lived in austerity and joylessness. A thankless, joyless life is an insult to God. We must be grateful for this physical life we lead, for life is a blessing and a privilege.

I know this truth. Admittedly, I was never as interested in physical exploits as my peers, who spent much of their youth running and wrestling to their heart's content. I found that marriage, too, passed me by. I was not really drawn to women in that way. My first love was, and is, the Church, and I have never felt lonely, not even in my dotage.

We don't examine the wonder that is our physical life because we are unable to recall any different way of being. Some of us may have fleeting memories or experience of the spiritual realms. Mostly though, we just continue along in our physical world unaware of any other state of existence.

God has created us equipped to enjoy a physical life. He has created wonderful and unique vessels for each of us – different genders and capacities, able-bodied or otherwise – and we are all ideally created for our Spirit's journey through the physical realm, the school of life on Earth. Let no-one tell you otherwise. Let no-one diminish the perfection of God's creation that is you. God loves us all. We are all of God, and we are all equal, leper or not, and we are all perfect in our imperfection.

Our human bodies, our costumes, are well-fitted for our individual journey through life where we are to be tested and tested again. Do not be fooled or coerced into thinking you are less worthy than another. Remember the words of Jesus and treat everyone with equal reverence, for you may be hosting Angels in disguise!

Do not let people pull you down. Rise above and remember God's love of all creation. Love yourself, love your God, and love all others and all God's creatures. Yes, this is hard to fathom in the times we live, where barbarity rules and life is hard, but it is the fundamental premise of life. If we fail to grasp this basic tenet, what purpose do we serve? We cannot live a righteous life and kill and maim and cause untold suffering. We must not give in to the lowest of our natures, the beast within. We must rise above. Oh, holy night, must I sing this message from the rooftops?

Yes, I am weary now, but there is still much to be done. The message is gathering, the Word has wings and has taken flight. Many flock to our churches now to hear the Word of God, and to understand the life of Jesus Christ and the message he provided.

The politics of late disturb my routine too often now. Politics of power, greed, hate, and spite – what loathsome combinations. A lethal partnering of all that is anathema to the Soul. Violence, bloodshed, betrayal, and treachery – they all leave the blackest hearts, the bloodiest legacies. No sooner one gone than replaced with another powerbroker more brutal than the last.

The security and sanctuary of the church is no guarantee in times of trouble and unrest. When the harvest is blighted and the people are hungry, there is no room in an empty stomach to entertain God. There is no thought of an afterlife when the here and now is so demanding. Daily needs are at the forefront of our existence – sustenance, shelter, safety. For many, there is no desire to examine the contents of their hearts when their larder is empty.

A brutalised and subjugated populace is not the way to inspire Godliness of Spirit. They must come willingly to rest in God's Sanctuary of Light, driven by the need for understanding of the purpose of their life and their eternal journey on the road to their salvation.

They are hungry, indeed. The free, but often stale loaves of bread the church provides are clearly not enough. Perhaps some more food may do the trick? Some soup perhaps? Warm sustenance for their bodies as the Word provides the sustenance for their Souls. Will the church coffers allow this extravagance, I wonder? Some of the rich among us may not take kindly to providing further funds to the church. If not for these benefactors, I myself would likely starve. I ponder the words I will use to prod them into action. Guilt or compassion, what tool is best to use to softly nudge them in the right direction? I am certain their Soul will be thankful, regardless.

The poor, of course, are considered the unfortunate detritus of life; worker bees and army fodder, expendable and replaceable, no free will to call their own. The rich despise them yet require them all the same. Who else to measure their success by?

The poor will be with us always, I suspect. The homeless, the feeble, the infirm, the destitute – such a large proportion of our world – swilling at our feet, bundled on doorsteps, dying in alleyways; such misery to be sure. If we don't see them, if we refuse to notice them, does our apathy diminish them? Or does their cloak of invisibility surround and protect them, inuring them to our averted gaze? We turn a blind eye as we step over them. We walk on by, ignoring their plight, turning our heads from the gore and horror of the farmyard of life. We refuse to acknowledge their humanity and their divinity as a creation of God; eternal Spirits living a physical existence on Earth. Oh, the inhumanity! Why do we turn away?

SUSTENANCE FOR OUR SOULS.

*We are all in this sea of humanity together, so
grab the oars, bail for your lives, and no-one
need go overboard!*

Destitution is confronting, to be sure, and is a stark
reminder of the inequality of our world. But we do the poor
and downtrodden justice by first and foremost acknowledg-
ing the truth of their existence. Remove their cloak of invisibility and lay witness to the grandeur of their Soul, for no-one
is immune to the vagaries of life. We, too, may one day find
our fortunes plummet.

Chicken soup, yes! Soup to go with the crusts of bread currently on offer, that will help in these times of growing inequality, where the gap between the richest and the poorest
among us just continues to get wider. I will feed their bodies
and nourish their Souls, just as Jesus would have wanted.
Indeed, it was he who said: 'Be kind to the least of us, and you
are kind to me'. I must remind the benefactors of this. Those
who hold the purse-strings must be coaxed to loosen their
grasp. They have more than enough to go around.

*Mankind's bubble is set to burst; the
champagne is for sharing!*

I sigh a sigh of the eternally wearied and hasten in my
work. Notes to make, action to take, no better time than the
present. The fire is again low. I stoke the flames and stare into

the abyss. My God, please guide me as your loyal servant to carry out your will. I am weary, no doubt, but ever willing to live a life of service. Please give me a sign that I am fulfilling my true purpose and have not let you down.

The candle flickers, then extinguishes itself. A sign, yes, I am redeemed! I feel blessed and secure in the knowledge that I am on the right path. This warms my heart and a peace descends. A gentle, loving warmth envelops me, and my heart expands. I am, by now, used to this spiritual energy when the Heavenly realms feel close. It really does feel as if the Angels embrace me.

May peace be with you always and may the Chariot of Time land upon the precipice of worry and doubt and whisk you away to new beginnings, where the truth will set you free.

Tears roll down my cheeks and the grace of everlasting love and joy surrounds me. I am loved, I am secure, and I am never alone. I am one with God who leads me from the wilderness and inspires me always. His is a gentle, loving hand that guides me onwards, ever upwards, on the journey of my Soul.

This journey of my life is one of many lives, of this I am sure. I know this truth. I feel it in my bones. The many visions that preceded this knowledge shook me to the core. I have a knowing, an understanding that this is as it has always been. I have had many lives, many chances to do the work of God. We all have many attempts to live a righteous life and progress closer to the pristine and glorious light of God.

The rich, naturally, deny this truth. Not all, of course, but many say their wealth and power is deserved, they do not wish to start again from scratch! If only they knew that the Wheel of Life is ever turning, they might give up their seats to someone more deserving. We all have a ticket to ride. We all wait in queue for the ride of our lives and we all take our turn at the top of the wheel. The wheel keeps turning and many bodies litter the ground below.

Look up to the Heavens and see the light shining brightly as the stars come out to play. Honour the truth of your existence and the ride of your life will be smooth and harmonious. Do not live a life of greed and envy. Do not push others from their seats. The day will come when you will view your life from Heaven above and understand your folly.

Oh dear, I'm drifting into sermon mode now. Yes, that will do the job for my next lecture – the Wheel of Life, greed, and the need to share our bounty – a perfect address to set the wheels in motion for my renewed plan to feed the hungry. The beggars are taking over the streets like never before.

It must be said, without a doubt, that it is greed, not wealth, that is the problem. We have many wealthy and generous benefactors. There are some, however, whose generosity is in equal proportion to the number of witnesses to such grand gestures. They secretly despise being deprived of their gold and silver and do it just for show. Indeed, wealth is never a problem in God's eyes, it is greed and apathy that lets mankind down. There are so many tests of life for the rich and the greedy, two separate but overlapping categories.

The masterpiece of life is applying the finishing touches. The banquet of the Soul, the divine buffet of life, is a feast of delight. New dishes are served, and many come to understand to share and share alike.

Ah, the small comforts of life in old age. A fire, wine, my precious cat 'Fallow', a warm bed, and cheese and bread enough to see me through the long, cold nights. To be left alone with my thoughts – what bliss! There are thoughts to divulge, and there are thoughts to polish in my mind until they are shiny with wear, caressing and turning to the light to make sense of their purpose. Are they to share, or are they precious jewels to clasp on tight, meant for me and me alone?

I detect movement in the corner of my eye and a scurrying sound. My cat leaps to attention, then decides the effort is beyond him. He settles again to do what he does best, and sleeps.

Indeed, there are too many memories. My heart breaks at some. I see myself as a young man in a large cave where Jesus is addressing a crowd, a secret gathering. What a blessing to hear his words of truth, splendour, and simplicity. I recall my annoyance at the selfish crowd pushing and shoving, not letting everyone in to hear the truth of *all that is*.

I recall the energy of Jesus, there was such a presence of love emanating from him. He touched something deep inside me, something sacred and buried in my heart of hearts – the direct link to my Soul. My heart opened and I understood what I must do. I must spread the Holy Word of Christ. For Jesus knows those who understand him, and Jesus comes to those who wish to know him. So many scrolls to write; so much wisdom to impart.

My work as a Scribe was, and still is, a blessing. There were cherished moments, but dangerous ones too. I recall passing scrolls secretly in the crowded marketplace. My sleeves were ideal hiding spots, wide and loose, and I passed the wisdom on. All too soon the day came that the wisdom stopped. What a sorry state of mankind. It felt like time stood still. A hush fell upon the land, and the sorrow could be felt by all creatures, great and small. Inconsolable, but indefatigable. We soldier on, called to arms – the loving arms of Christ.

Purposefully I preach the good news to the masses; the good news that we are all eternal, and our Spirit never dies. It lives on, ready to do battle another day – the battle of free will, the battle of the ego, the battle with ourselves.

The followers scattered to all ends of the Earth, spreading the Word of God. They continued the work of Jesus with sorrow in their hearts and the pain of separation permeating their very being. We are all human with foibles and undesirable traits – jealousy, a temper too quick, impatience, a taste for fame and power. We all had weaknesses, each and every one of us.

I pause for a moment, my heart opening up as the memories flood in …..

……..Indeed, *she* was the best of us, the closest to Jesus and the wisest of us all. She understood his words when we sometimes struggled. She had patience to explain what we could not. The love between those two was not of this world. It was a story of love and loss, such pain for her Soul – a sacrificial journey for mankind – for she understood her role and she understood what Jesus must do. The tears, the pain, the sacrifice…. Dear Mary, you surrendered to your pain and gave your heart to the world. And the children of your union were exquisite in their spiritual beauty, with grace and wisdom beyond their years.

I digress. It was a long time ago, but the imprint of the pain still rendered raw on my heart is impossible to deny. Did I do enough, Jesus? You were in your prime and it all happened so quickly, there was not enough time to continue our work openly. Was I too caught up in my task as Scribe to appreciate how things would turn out? I was so young. Was I too self-centred, basking in my honourable role and the company I was keeping, to fully understand? Please forgive me, Jesus.

I am sorry and I am saddened that I didn't get to say goodbye. I know you visit me in my sleep. I know you guide my hand and my words when spreading the wisdom. I am thankful that you think I am still worthy of such an honour. I would kneel if my knees would bear it. I am so proud to have known you – to know you – and to tell your story to those who listen; the story of the wonder of the Christ Light as you came to save the world.

And I know you will come again. You said you would, but not until the time was right. I pray that the times will be changed enough for acceptance and reverence. Will mankind be up to the challenge? It worries me, Jesus, that all is not as it should be. Violence escalates, hunger abounds, but your memory does live on.

The Word spreads as you had intended, Jesus, and many come to hear your wisdom. The acceptance of the Scriptures is gaining ground in foreign lands. The Word is travelling further and further afield where many flock to hear your profound wisdom and messages of love and compassion to all. They want to know of the Kingdom of God which awaits our eternal Spirit, and the news of a kind God, a just God, who watches over us as we go about our lives. This truth is travelling far and wide!

> *The Whistler in his Den knows that truth*
> *is the wind of light that speaks of love and*
> *righteousness of being.*

Free will, of course, is the downfall of many. The wrong choices are made, and lives are lived in barbarity and hate. Life is cheap, horror abounds, and many do not understand the burdens on their Souls. Such heavy burdens, my Lord. Such darkness looming, I see it in their eyes. Ready to resort to violence in the blink of an eye, it is survival of the fittest and the fastest, no care or thought to the mild and meek among us. The darkness of Spirit gnaws. There is no respite for those who succumb to poor choices and bad deeds, just drunken sorrow that their lives offer no relief from the horror that surrounds them.

How is it that the sun continues to rise each day, oblivious to mankind's treacherous nightly forages? Life goes on with barely a blink from Mother Nature. Fools continue on their merry way, gallivanting along the road of perennial ignorance. But who am I to judge? I understand this truth... 'judge not, yet ye yourself be judged'. None of us is perfect, that much is clear, but it saddens me God, that some appear beyond redemption, in my eyes at least. Of course, I know that you love us all equally, but I feel that the cost of their transgressions must be a mighty load for their Soul to bear.

Forgive them, God. They understand not care nor compassion towards their fellow brothers and sisters. They take in greed and lust, and kill over trivialities. Such monstrous appetites for blood. The world is no better than how Jesus left it. Violence is rife, life is cheap, and many worship at the altars of greed and power. They venerate idols, show little mercy, and fail to understand the tests of life or the golden rule: 'Do unto others as you would have them do unto you.' They take this to mean they should unsheathe the blade first! This command goes up in smoke every time they pillage and burn. Such wasteful heartache and pain, on both sides of the sword.

My attention drifts. Come to me my dearest cat and let me give you warmth. A gentle touch, a rumbling purr – now that is the meaning of life right there. Love, trust, and security make a perfect brew for all God's creatures, such sublime sustenance for the Soul.

Time for rest now. Tomorrow I must meet my brethren and provide alms for the fallen. The many-sided populace who seek to know God's Word make up the truly pious and the truly humble, alongside the truly dreadful and, of course, the truly hungry! I grin to myself, confident that I minister to all without fear or favour.

Another day to do God's work, how privileged I am. God willing that I would wake again in the morning, and not be spirited away in my sleep. What a blessing that would be to see another dawn. (My constant oscillations on this point are clear to me, and hopefully, I trust, to God.) Besides, who would take over my work? Who is ready, who is able to do what must be done? Please God, give me a sign. They are all so young and yet so keen, but it's such a burden to be handed down. I shall sleep on it tonight.

Chapter 2

The heart hears what the mind does not.

❖

The day is clear and bright, and the crowds they are heaving. There is much activity, and bright colours adorn the market stalls. The streets are awash with the city folk conducting the business of daily life, with thieves and rascals lurking around each corner. I wind my way around the baskets of produce, piles of rags, and the rabid dogs.

Greetings to all, greetings of the morning! A nod here, a small wave there, I recognise my loyal brethren as I go about town. It is a city of hope, a city of promise; an ever-growing city with more and more willing and ready to embrace the Word of God.

Many hunger for the Gospels; they know there must be more to life than wretchedness and sorrow. They believe in God, Jesus, and the Holy Grail. They want to believe, they truly do. The message of love, so simple and so powerful, takes root and prospers.

THE HEART HEARS WHAT THE MIND DOES NOT.

*The flourishing vine is bearing fruit
and craning for the light.*

Prosperous, productive, and well-rooted – our work has paid off! The toil, the exhaustion, and the repetitive verses have all produced results. The large and growing congregations attest to that. The Word is gaining ground as the wisdom finds true home in the hearts and minds of the brethren. I sigh as I recall fondly the words delivered from Spirit in the night:

> *Deliver the news to save the world. The best is
> yet to come, dear friend, and the Holy Light
> will soothe you to your rest. The Word is what
> they want to hear and many a tune will fall on
> deaf ears. But persevere and you will see that
> the Light will shine, the Angels will sing, and the
> Word will settle in the arms of those who seek
> true purpose of their Souls. Praise be to God.*

The critics of the church would beg to differ. 'A church of lepers and old women, the weak and the poor, what use are they to God?' And so on, they blaspheme. 'What use is a God who gives nothing in return for their miserable piety but pain of life and hunger in its stead?'

If only they knew what was truly at stake, but the truth of the equality of our Souls is an abomination that many of the greedy and powerful cannot abide. They see themselves as being equal to their pagan gods in their offerings. It is a business partnership, for sure. Tit for tat, sacrifice for harvest, blood for battle glory. Their faith is nothing but an extraction, a deal, a bargaining of their aces. They do not bow down to their idols but, rather, pacify and deceive, with no love lost in the transactions they complete. They act with more fear than love, more deceit than humility, and more greed than grace. If only they understood that the one true God is a God of love, a God who requires nothing less than love – unconditional love for all.

My work has been productive. My followers are loyal devotees of the church. The brethren – many of them quite wealthy – mostly understand the need to give to those less fortunate. If not of their gold and silver, their time – time to ease the burdens of their neighbour. Time is a gift to bestow on those who are suffering. Time to listen, time to heal. Time to support, carry, clean, and cook. Time to help others in small ways and large.

Compassion and kindness are the cornerstones of Jesus' ministry. To aid the sick and the poor in whatever way possible is to grow your Soul with love. Your good intentions will carry you to your rest, at home with God the Father as he lays your burdens down and soothes your weary brow.

What an honour to be able to serve your fellow human being. To recognise the humanity and divinity of each and every one of us is no easy feat when divisions are rife and cruelty to the 'other' is a horror borne of man. We are all equal, of this I am sure, and I am no closer to God than the street sweeper, the goat herder, or the criminal at the gate. I understand God's love for mankind, but this does not put me ahead in his favour.

THE HEART HEARS WHAT THE MIND DOES NOT.

*Behold the might of destiny's shadow, for the
firefly and the gadfly are one and the same –
creatures of God awash with his love.*

Have no doubt, we are all equal in our Maker's presence.
Some of us are just closer to the truth of God's divine love
for all of his creation. Rest assured the time for love is now.
There can never be too much love. There can never be too
much bread and honey wine either! All of these things are the
staples of life. Sustenance for all, we wither away when these
staples are lacking.

*A heart with no love goes black on the
vine of life.*

To survive and thrive we must give love; unconditional
love to all. Even the lepers and the prostitutes – considered
by many as the detritus of life – are worthy of love, yet they
are treated as vermin by the authorities, the powers that be.
If only they knew how swiftly the tables of life can be turned
asunder. The judge becomes the judged, and the cycle of life
conspires to throw the cats among the pigeons.

Of course, my dear brethren, you are too concerned with
this life to worry about the next. Survival of the physical often
takes precedence over the spiritual. That I do understand.
Fear not that your physical needs become you. Intend to do
what's right and holy. Intend to live with unconditional love to
all, joy in your heart, and forgiveness of all who have wronged
you, and your Spirit is served.

Love each other and love yourself. That is the recipe of

life. Treat others as you yourself would wish to be treated, and love will see you through the dark days of winter. Love will feed your Soul. Let God take care of the rest.

> *The fruit of the vine grows heavy with*
> *the nectar of love.*

Serve your Spirit the blessings of life and you will prosper. Serve blessings of the heart and Soul and answer the dutiful call of life. It is the duty of the righteous to understand their true purpose, to spread love and light to all others in their wake and await the return of Christ.

The heart hears what the mind does not. The heart opens up to the understanding that is innate; the knowing that the Christ Light will heal all our sorrow and pain. It will salve the misery of mankind. How we all hunger for Christ and his sacred light. The Christ will return, I know this to be true. Oh, how we await the bloom of life, Heaven-sent, to waken us from our dream-state. To help us open up to all that is pure and holy, and the grace of God in all its glory!

I am reminded of a verse received from Spirit; such beautiful confirmation of what mankind's future holds:

The Light of Christ the Redeemer returns

> *The wings of the Dove will alight at dawn.*
> *The blessed and the true will sing the tune of true*
> *surrender to our Lord.*
> *All will be revealed.*
> *All is known, the way is clear.*

THE HEART HEARS WHAT THE MIND DOES NOT.

The energy is building.
In time's great worry it stands complete with
wisdom of the Ages.

The wise are ready, the trumpets blare.
Such music for the masses.
A spectacle of love and light.
A show so grand that all who witness know such
love, such joy to be revealed.
Come into the parlour of understanding, spread
the good news,
and understand that all is in its place.
Let the Light Show begin!

———

Be patient dear ones, we have much to do and much to learn to prepare the world once more. Will planet Earth survive the hate of mankind? Such bloodshed and agony; fallen monuments of mankind. Cruelty and barbarity lead the way to heartache evermore. Is this the legacy of Christ? Not so, we strive to play our part and the lean, mean days of thunder in the night-sky will abate for another day. The churning, burning agony of life will settle anew into a gentle rhythm of love and harmony for all. That is the future as I see it.

Is it too much to believe that mankind will one day see the error of their ways and set a new trajectory towards sanctity of all God's creatures on Earth? Believe me when I tell you this: the past will heal, and the imprint of futures known will bring us to our knees.

Our way ahead is joyous anticipation! Ah, to be young again and savour the fruits of thy endeavours. The heart beats proudly, aware of how far we have come in educating the masses. Each new day is a blessing for the Soul, a chance to live in harmony and grace and await the new day dawning.

A camel understands the load is great, but
greater still the hope for a new tomorrow, when
burdens are lifted, and the sands of time flow
swiftly through the hourglass of your intentions.

———

I stop at a market stall in quiet reverie, not quite remembering how I got here. "*Good day to you, my friend. Time is of the essence today. I need ink and parchment, and a quill if you please.*" Best not to be caught short late at night when the Word is flowing, and supplies are dwindling. The trader grabs my hand and kisses it, and I patiently abide this greeting of respect, much as it discomfits me. My ornate ring of gold and precious gems represents the holy church of God, and I neither really own it, nor borrow it. Rather, I belong to it and it belongs to me. It is worn as a sacred adornment, a token of my holy authority, and my priestly attire delights the onlookers as they seek to place me on a spiritual pedestal.

In truth, if they saw me naked without my plain, but pristine, robe and my sacred jewellery, they would be disappointed for sure. They would, no doubt, believe that clothes do maketh the man. Without my priestly armour I would simply be an old man of flesh and bone – wrinkled, weak, and sagging – a direct contrast to the righteous power of the Holy Spirit that I represent. I would stand naked in all my glory as a creation of God, the weakness and morbidity of the flesh being no match for the supreme glory of our Spirit self. Our Spirits are so light, so pure, and ageless. The youthful eternity of the Spirit is a wonder to behold.

What a blessing to discard our old bodies. Young or old, no matter, nothing compares to the freedom of Spirit. We discard our latest costume of life without a hankering for the fashion of the past. Our Spirit self looks ever onwards, ever upwards to the light. Once in the Spirit realms we patiently await our next fitting, ready for the next great role of our lives in the theatre of our redemption that is Earth.

Faith is the robe best worn daily, not just when the harsh, cold reality of life starts to bite.

Our Spiritual and Angelic audience looks on, fans of our performance, cheering us on from the sidelines. What a show! What a masterful display! No dress rehearsals are allowed. Each part is the performance of our lives, and we get to review each and every performance when we return to Spirit. We hope upon hope that we fulfilled our part and did not drift too far from the script we agreed to read from, or from the role we signed up to play when we planned our incarnation. Reincarnation is an unfashionable truth I know, but the truth, nonetheless.

Honour all parts in the pantomime of life. Everyone has a purposeful life, a reason for being, and a lesson to learn, no matter how inconsequential you think their part may be.

Honour the journey of their Soul.

*Each to their own..... a pathway is sown, a map
is known, and all will find true peace in the
beginnings of true surrender to their Soul.*

I wind my way past the many hawkers selling their wares. The beggars, so forlorn in their misery, barely raise an upwards glance at the passing procession of buyers and sellers. Such a display of humanity abounds. There are goat herders, farmers, mothers with babes in arms, thieves, drunkards, and prostitutes. A large, unkempt group of soldiers is milling around, kicking stones whilst waiting on new commands to be issued. The crowd parts a little to let me through. They would not dare hijack a Man of God, I believe, nevertheless I clutch my purchases tightly under my cape. Such precious commodities – ink and parchment. It is such a blessing to be literate.

I bless my parents every day for the honour of my birth, and I bless my wonderful grandparents who were so loving and wise. They ensured I had the right tools at my disposal to make something of my life. To read and write is a privilege in this world. And it is an honour and a privilege to be a witness to the journey of Jesus and the love he came to share with the world. Nothing else comes close to the joy I feel in passing this wisdom on. It is the purpose of my life. A Scribe of God is the role I was born to do.

The life of Jesus was a life of compassion, healing, love, and wisdom. He truly showed us how to live. He embodied truth and grace; his divinity became him. He was gentle, kind, and wise, and I so wish that I could emulate him. I am ashamed now to say that, at first, I did not fully understand the sacrificial role he took on. Things moved so quickly there was barely time to ponder how it would all end, or when it would all end. Why did it end so soon? We were barely started on our journey.

Jesus knew what he must do, and Mary understood this truth. We others lagged behind. The Magdalene energy of love and compassion supported Jesus with his burden. And it was a burden to be sure, but it was also a gift, and he took his mission on with strength and righteousness. Mary supported Jesus in his mission and carried his wisdom forward. She helped us with our pain, and we were ecstatic with the news that he lived on.

We knew Jesus, and so we loved him, for to know him was to love him. There was no other way but love. He was the essence of love in all his glory and the light shone brightly from the depths of his heart, his compassion a guiding light for all to follow. What say you when freedom holds your hand and challenges you to understand the true purpose of your life? Do you grasp the task with both hands, or retreat and hide?

Faith is the hunger of the Soul to rise above your daily grind that is life on Earth and reach to greater heights. Faith anchors you to a Port of Love, where the storms of life cannot shake you from your moorings.

Free will is a choice of both the brave and the broken-hearted. We all have choices to make. We can take the high road or the low road: the detour leading nowhere, or the elevated pathway to the higher vibration of love. There are no shortcuts on the pathway to enlightenment. It takes hard work and perseverance to live in righteousness and truth. Trust that you make the right choices because your choices are with you for evermore. Choose love over hate, wisdom over ignorance, generosity of Spirit over greed and spite, and you will be redeemed.

To all believers comes a time when a choice is
in the air. Stand tall and true, remove all doubt,
and the rest is up to God.

Prayer is righteous. Prayer is masterful. Pray regularly, as this will connect you to the Heavenly vibration of God. And it is this, your own personal connection to God, that is the most important aspect of your faith.

I feel a prayer forthcoming:

Blessed Spirit, Hosanna in the highest.
The Holy Grail of life seeks to see our mission
done.
So we return forthwith in goodness and grace to
your loving arms once more.
Our task complete, we understand that life is a
chance to grow our Souls with love.

And grow we do, when we deliver what we came
for – grace and righteousness of being, delivered
to the doorway of our Soul.
Hallelujah, we salute you.
Upon the Holy Altar of Love and Light is the
recognition that we are on our pathway to
eternal salvation.
And we will not be thwarted in our quest to feast
at your Holy Table.
The universe is calling, and all our good deeds
lead the way and sing our praises home.
The Blessed and the Holy know that theirs is a
harmony worth singing and sharing with the
world.

After a few visits with the faithful I arrive back at the church in time for a late lunch. A simple meal of bread and stew has been lovingly prepared by my housekeeper. I have simple tastes. Old age determines that my stomach has the final say on my delicate constitution.

I hurriedly eat and prepare for the coming short prayer meeting. I sit quietly, preparing key phrases in my mind, like a road map in case I falter. I have been doing this role for so long now that I am rarely nervous. The church is my home, and it is the only place I truly feel at ease. To walk the streets is no doubt a greater test of faith, as danger lurks in every shadow that leaps across my path.

When preaching the Word of God, the reverence of the

duty overcomes me and I truly become a holy vessel, an old man in a robe no longer. It is such a holy service to foster righteousness of being in others. I can see the light in the eyes of those who take my message on. Others look confused, or weary, or uncomfortable at best, squirming in their seats or trying not to snore. Many, many moons ago this would have irritated me greatly, but now I understand that the vessel is weak. It is feat enough to arrive in one piece and stay the course, let alone be fully present in both mind and body. Sometimes, I, too, wish to be elsewhere. In the arms of the Angels, no less!

Some of the traders are missing from church, I notice. Likely caught up in the hive of activity about town as the idolaters prepare for some annual parade or other, the name of which escapes me now. A festival of the damned, no doubt; some pagan barbarity to fan the flames of debauchery and violence. Oh dear, I fear my cloak of righteousness and grace has slipped right off my shoulders! May the Lord grant me patience to understand these primitive rituals, and the forbearance to judge not, lest I, too, be judged.

We cannot escape our human condition, of course. Indeed, it is our humanness that allows us to be tested in life. It is the means for us to rise to all the challenges that living a human life entails – birth and death, sickness and health, misery and joy, love and hate. To go through life with no faith in a greater purpose is a lonely journey indeed, a confusing journey where nothing about the human condition makes sense. Oh, the hardship. Such inequality!

We must understand that all our lives have a divine purpose, and we will be tested no matter the circumstances of our lives. Rich, poor, humble, proud – we are all tested. And we pass our tests if we live in righteousness of Spirit always, no matter our pain or suffering. Indeed, *because of, and in spite of*, our pain and suffering. Humility and grace, joy of life, forgiveness, and unconditional love of all – these rules are non-negotiable. These are our tests, conditional on our surrender to God's will. And with each life we lead we progress our Soul with wisdom, no matter how short our life or how we may have failed our tests. Wisdom and growth are assured.

> *For each of our lives adds to the wisdom of our Soul, our accumulated library of both the victor and the vanquished.*

Remember, it is our 'intention' that is key. If we intend to always act in goodness and in grace and lead a life of unconditional love to all, a life of service, a life of sacrifice to those less fortunate, then we have found the key to our salvation. If we act with hateful spite, greed, and loathing whilst pretending to be righteous, our Soul looks on, disappointed and shrivelled. And all will be recorded in our Record Book of Life – a lone scorecard of hypocrisy and sorrow, adrift in the wilderness of a wasteland of chances.

How do I see thee?

I understand the wisdom Jesus came to Earth to share, to demonstrate a life lived in selfless acts of kindness and grace, untold healing miracles, and faith in God's love for all. I have seen and heard things that others may doubt, but faith is the muscle you must exercise daily. Have faith in the divine scheme of things. Have faith that you are loved and precious. Understand that you are here to learn lessons in the school of life on Earth and to progress your Soul with love. Elevate to the higher vibration of love and light in every thought, word, and action, and truly bring the divine light of Heaven to Earth. This is enlightenment. This is your purpose in life, your reason for being. This is the meaning of life.

To gain enlightenment is to understand that you are one with God and you are a powerful creator in your own right. You create the circumstances of your life by your thoughts, words, and actions. Create, and the universe will respond. Nothing is random. God's love is not random. He loves us all, no matter our transgressions on the pathway of our Soul.

Faith allows you to let go of all that ails you
and 'let God'. It is a sublimation to the divine
plan, a realisation that you are part of God
and he is part of you – the interconnectedness of
faith and love and the universe and all
God's creatures in it.

Resist the urge to bargain with your Soul, just tell it as it is. Nowhere to run or hide, the Book of Life sees all, records all. You cannot bribe, trick, or deceive your way to glory. All is known by God the Father, Creator of Heaven and Earth.

Some may believe they are favoured by God, and that their fame, power, or wealth is deserved because they are special, more worthy, harder working, or cleverer than most. They fail to understand that the tests still come thick and fast and they cannot escape their call to grace, or their fall from grace, if they ignore their chance to make a difference in the world.

The powerful have the means to change the life of many. Is this a test too far? They have many tests, many chances, to grow their Soul with love of all humanity.

The powerful have a mighty chance to show what
they are made of; a mighty ship to turn around
and send lifeboats out to all.

Beware the grasp of envy that seeks to hold on tight. Beware the fools who spend their lives bringing others down, causing misery and sorrow as the poison spreads around. They fail to love themselves. To love God, you must first love yourself. Self-loathing is a suit that repels all love and grace; a suit of armour, ill-fitting and heavy, to block out all the light. Remove this protective coating and see what you do find. Examine the reason for your pain and offer it up to God. Heal and the world heals with you.

To forsake and be forsaken; the lesson of the Ages
comes home to roost in mankind's Soul.

Chapter 3

How do I count the ways?

❖

How do I know thee?

I look into the heart of mankind as I look into my own heart. I plumb the depths, searching in the treasure chest of love, pain, and sorrow of the deep. What jewels I find there! Memories of yesteryear, boyhood dreams, disappointments, and pain that never sleeps – the pain of remembrance of the horrors borne of mankind. The violence, the cruelty, the barbarity, and the sorrow, but also the love, the resurrection, the joy, the upliftment, and the unity of God's grace for all! This is the knowledge that completes us. How blessed we are to know that we are Spirit living a human existence and our destiny is not of this world.

Do not forget that we are eternal and return to God forthwith, taking our Earthly baggage along for the ride, our baggage of human foibles and bad choices. We carry these burdens to the end of our days unless we release them with love and transmute them for all time, with love and forgiveness forever in our hearts.

HOW DO I COUNT THE WAYS?

Help others with their burdens. They are impossibly heavy to carry alone, and many are laden high and wide. Teach them to forgive, to let go and release the pain that anchors them to their grief – their grief of life. To forgive all others and forgive themselves, this is the road they must take. Their baggage of surrender will become light as a wisp, and their joy will be the energy that surrounds them on their journey to the light of God's Kingdom.

I know this truth. I, too, have succumbed to hatred of the other. I, too, understand the richness of emotion, the satisfying thickness of the energy flowing towards the wedged object of your antipathy, leaving self-righteous superiority and anger in its wake.

It took me many moons – perhaps years – to truly forgive the persecutors of Jesus. I now understand it was meant to be. They were playing a part, a free will choice they made to turn their back on love and all that was good and holy. If not them, others would have stepped in to take their place. There was no shortage of those seeking power over others, willing to choose pain and sorrow over compassion and grace.

I forgave them, as Jesus forgave them. I understand that they were tested in their choices, just as we are tested in our choice to forgive or to hold on tight to the pain that wakes us in our beds. Non-forgiveness of those who cause you pain is a sure-fire way to increase your pain ten-fold.

Non-forgiveness corrodes your Soul and leaves
your heart withering in the shadows of a life
lived as though it were trapped in stasis. There
is no progression to be had, no wisdom to be

gained. It is a life frozen in the icicles of winter –
a tundra of the Soul.

I have seen the joy as the light of spring thaws a frozen heart. I have seen true liberty as chains are loosened and hearts are opened, as the object of your hate is released from the prison of your mind. Such lightness of being sets the way for true conversion of your Soul.

I know this. I have lived it and I have seen it in others many times. The followers of Christ knew to lay their burdens down. Much angst, much sorrow led them to this point, where to maintain the rage was to deny Jesus' plan for all of us. Jesus forgave all, even the ungodly – the murderers, the cruel wielders of unjust and untold brutality, the greedy and the corrupt – and he offered eternal redemption for our Souls. Who am I to defy the example that he set for us? Who am I to go it alone in carrying hate and spite with me to my grave? It is such a torturous burden for the Soul.

Resist the urge to plot revenge. Resist the urge to nurture hate and non-forgiveness all your days and nights, and you will be redeemed. This is the way of the Lord.

The fruit on the vine requires tender loving care
and pruning of that which does not serve.

Oh Jesus, how your divine love sustains me. It sustains us all. You are the light of our lives, the holiest of holy. You are the light that leads us Heaven bound. We aspire to be humble, loving, virtuous, and wise, just as you yourself set the example of how we should live our lives.

The people are pining for love and grace in their lives. The meaning of their lives, and of your life, are intertwined, but they think of you as separate from all mankind. Then comes the day they pass over and finally realise that there is no division. The veil is thin, and you were here with us in Spirit all along!

We are one and we are many, and our true self understands the truth of life. We are all connected, and we are all equal in Spirit. There is no division based on race, gender, or creed. There is no division between Heaven and Earth. And every day in every way, you are with us always.

A hush descends upon the faithful, and a woman steps forward in rags. She drops to her knees and begs forgiveness for her sins. *"There, there, dear child. God forgives all, but you must also forgive yourself. Go now and forever pray with gratitude and grace, for you have found your salvation here in this church of the one true God of love and forgiveness. You are always welcome. You are always loved. You are always forgiven. There is always a place for you here."*

This church is a sanctuary for all those who wish to know the Word of God. But it is not enough to have this knowledge, you must practice it daily. You must live and breathe it. You must hold it dear to your heart and let it define your very essence of being. Let the Word become you. In the beginning was the Word, and the Word is God. God is love, and the Word is Love. *Love is.*

Love must be at the forefront of every choice you make. For

every decision you need make, the answer is love. It is always love that will salve your heart of the pain and emptiness of life. Love all unconditionally and the universe responds.

The proof is in the pudding and the pudding
does bear fruit.

Jesus taught us selfless love, and his gift will be with us always. Love yourself, no matter your transgressions, as Jesus loves you dearly. He loves you when you forget to love yourself. He loves you when you refuse to love yourself, for Jesus is the supreme beacon of love and light. He came to Earth to show us how to prosper. And prosper we will. Our Souls will be the recipients of the gift of love and righteousness of being.

Prosperous is the way of the Lord – prosperity of Spirit. Do not confuse this with material prosperity, that is worthless to you in the Kingdom of Heaven. Give what you can to the poor and you will see that the hand that gives, outstretched in love, is the hand to lead you home. Home to God's Kingdom where the Angels do sing your glory.

Once upon a time God said to thee…..*open your arms, your minds, your purse to the poor, and your life will be prosperous beyond imagining…..* All who care for those less fortunate will find the fortune of the Soul. Blessings will be upon you in God's great garden of Earth, and your name will be emblazoned on the Honour Roll of Life, where all good students aspire to be.

Take note that the carriage awaits those who selflessly help others with no expectations in return, for that is truly honourable. The carriage of antiquity will carry you to your rest, and you will delight in the knowledge that you did your best, you passed the grade, and your Soul is in ecstasy of the light to set you free.

Many regret their life lived in selfishness and greed. Many regret that they failed to understand that they could live another way. Have no regrets. Let your life be purposeful as you travel the pathway of your Soul and show Jesus what you have learned.

The giver of love is a light on the horizon of hope.

I often wonder whether my words get through to those who need to hear them the most. It seems to me that the brethren who do the most charitable deeds are the ones who probably can least afford it. Is it perhaps because they understand the vagaries of life and are not so far removed from those less fortunate? They know the tables could be turned in an instant and there is often no less than a basket of bread that separates them from the hungry at the banquet of life.

I stop after mass to nod and speak with those who wish to know me. Many have agreed to fund soup for the hungry, as they have seen with their own eyes the hunger that is encroaching on the city. Impossible to ignore, it stifles true enjoyment of their own palate. I am pleased with their reaction to my pleas but know that their resolve may only last until they step outside the door and ignore the first beggar lying prostrate at their feet. Once back to the daily grind of life they have little time for merciful ponderings or their shield may well crack wide apart, exposing them to the heartbreak and injustice of the cruel inequalities of life.

—∞—

My dear Jesus, how do I count the ways?
A short prayer comes to mind:

The beatification of Christ

How do I love thee, Lord?
I love thee as the ground does swell and Mother
Nature erupts in full glory.
I love thee as the night-time brings a hush upon
the dawn.
I love thee as my heart does sing when the power
of your song moves me.
I love thee as the sun does rise, and shines upon
my Soul.

Chapter 4

A word to the wise.

❖❖❖

Christ the Redeemer offers redemption for our Soul. For we are human, and we are tested. No-one on this Earth is perfect, but we learn by our mistakes and we progress our Souls with love. We strive, we learn, and thus we prosper.

The Word is travelling far and wide. Many devout believers are learning, by rote, the story of Jesus and the truth he came to share. The Word sustains them, and that is all good and well, as parchment is costly, and the Scribes cannot keep pace with the demand for the Scriptures. But let me remind you, my dear brothers and sisters of Christ, that learning by rote does not absolve one from acting by rote. And by this, I mean acting in accordance with the Word in all we say and do, every day and in every way. 'Knowing' and 'acting' do not always measure up, as well we all know. As children, we know not to eat too much sweet honey cake but still we sicken with bellyache.

There is much power in knowing the Word. The power of knowing the correct way to live our lives, in righteousness and truth, serves our Spirit with love. We are elevated to the higher spiritual vibration, closer to the divine light of God the Father. And we are empowered with the knowledge that we are free to make this choice. Our free will defines us. Our free will also binds us.

We must not use our knowledge of the Word, or our ability for rote recital of the Scriptures, as rationale to act 'holier than thou' and step upon the pedestal. Do not take the name of God in vain. We are God's simple servants. Do not cite your knowledge of the Word as belief that you are chosen, superior to all others, and that you are favoured as a messenger of God.

It is a false prophet who metes out God's Word in dribs and drabs and fails to feed the hungry masses the spiritual sustenance from above. Starvation rations will not do! This knowledge must be shared with all, far and wide, not cloistered away by priests and holy men and women who believe such knowledge must be earned. They argue it is too precious to be shared around like leavened bread but, rather, doled out in piecemeal crumbs, more easily digested by the masses who are always left hungering for more.

The Kingdom of Heaven belongs to all. No-one has a priority ticket. No-one gets to push ahead of the queue by virtue of privilege, literacy, studiousness, or station in life. These are many fine qualities, to be sure, but great volumes recited by rote will impress no-one if good deeds are *in absentia*. Eschew the compulsion to regurgitate biblical references to all you meet. The competition in this life is solely with oneself; to rise above adversity and live purely from the heart centre.

Make this life your best life yet in glorious adherence to the Word of God; a life of simplicity, unconditional love, joy, and forgiveness to all. This is the competition of your life. It is not a race to power and status against all others, rather, it is a competition with your shadow self, your ego, who seeks to sabotage your life.

Overcome any desire to live in pompous disdain
of those you deem less knowledgeable. Knowledge
is not wisdom. Greed and vanity will see your
good works undone.

Jesus was humble, and all who knew him knew that the power of his presence was his love for all mankind. He sacrificed much for us so that we would 'know the way'. His memory sustains us. We wander no longer in the wilderness, aimless and in pain, remembering a sorrow that has no name. We are renewed and nourished with the knowledge that Jesus came to relieve us of our burdens, our heavy burdens that lay our Soul to waste.

Jesus showed us how to live a virtuous life in harmony and grace; to love each other, to love ourselves, and to love our God. Simplicity of life in all its splendour. To live our best life with compassion to all, and let no grudge define us; this is the way of the Lord. No ill-will, spite, or hate need burden our Souls once more. We forgive all others and we forgive ourselves, and thus enjoy the privilege of being alive once more in the school of life on Earth. Praise be to God.

The Christ is risen. The Christ will come again. This much is known, is understood, for when we stand as one, in holiness and grace, the future is assured. Jesus will light the way and all our days will be fruitful with the knowledge of our Souls;

the eternal knowledge gathered thus far on our journey of
surrender to the light.

> *Delight in all that comes your way, for the*
> *dewdrop and the rain dance in delightful*
> *harmony. Heaven sent, the light will shower you*
> *in glory and all will be well with the world. The*
> *dewdrop and the rain unite, the melody of joy*
> *and forgiveness is a never-ending chorus, the*
> *tune a blessing to the world.*

Never again will mankind wander in the spiritual wilderness of life. When we are ready, when the way is prepared, Jesus
will grace us once more. This time the world will be ready.
This time, after many moons in the wilderness, mankind will
see past greed and power, and understand that love is the key
to greatness of Spirit. Love is the way to retrieve lost hope and
glory. Love is the equation that adds up to righteousness of
being. Love is.

> *Be strong in your wisdom, pure in your faith and*
> *keen in your love of all, and you will see that*
> *destiny's ride is a joyous mount and happiness*
> *will be your steed.*

And when Jesus comes once again to show us the way,
there will be no hate, apathy, or neglect of the unfortunate
amongst us, just love and compassion will see us on our way.
Jesus will know how far we have travelled on the journey of
our Souls. He will look into our hearts and declare:

A WORD TO THE WISE.

*You have come a long way mankind. You dance
upon the glories of the day with love in your
hearts and wisdom in your Souls. You have seen
the worst of days and the best of days. And best
of all, you have understood my good works and
the Word; the means to set you free from the
tyranny of all that is sorrowful. I adore you and
I forgive you, and all is well with the world. My
children, I salute you.*

With the service now ended, I meet with the keeper of the
purse who tells me of his plan to put into action my request
for increased sustenance for the hungry. I leave the minutiae
to him, for he is trustworthy and has honourable brethren to
assist. There is much honour in feeding the poor – honour at
the Table of Love, honour to feed the Soul – for compassion
is the means to rise above our daily woes and understand the
trials and tribulations of others less fortunate. The perspec-
tive of empathy is a means to rise above all bigotry and apathy
and step into the shoes of others, if only for a moment.

*To wear the gown of the downtrodden is to
understand that life is hard, but harder still when
cruelty bears upon them like a
hawk upon a dove.*

I return to my room and replace my clean robe with
my old, dusty brown one. I settle down to refreshments of

pomegranates, bread and honey, such beautiful nourishment from God's great garden. I reflect on my words this day. Was I clear? Was I impatient? Repetitive or meandering? I guess I may never really know the truth. No-one, not even my most trusted confidantes would likely tell me straight at this grand old age. They would probably just wait it out, knowing that I'll not likely last much longer, and better to suffer boredom than assail my pride. They really are fond of me, I muse, as I am of them. Many have been with me for tens of years, and I truly give them my praises. For we have all travelled a long way, we have learned a lot and have seen much hardship and suffering. We have lost so many dear friends, and look forward to meeting them again in eternity, our Soul group reunited.

Our lives have been productive, although there is always so much more we could do. The Scribes find it difficult to keep up with the demand, and I feel as if time is against us. Have I done enough? Old age slows me down. I do not get out and about as much as I used to. The pagan rites seem to have taken on new fervour in this city. There are many more followers, new settlers in town, that are injecting new life into the pagan rituals of old. I have seen them around the streets, inciting others with their masks and incantations.

I tended to ignore these pagan ceremonies at first, believing them to be harmless manifestations of a bygone era, resurrected in popularity in times of hardship and blighted harvests. But now, I am not so sure. Indeed, there are many stories emerging of violence and terror, inflamed by drunkenness and debauchery after many such gatherings. It appears to me these behaviours are simply drunken revelry in disguise, under cover of religious fervour and propriety and in deference to such gods who are said to revel in the frenzied excitement of the masses. Their wickedness becomes them. But what would I know? I am old and out of touch with the young, I fear.

Still, what do they want that this church cannot provide them? Yes, I do know the answer, and I sigh with the wisdom of my years. They want instant gratification in this life – riches, power, and recognition – not the distant, intangible promise of eternal salvation. Foolish? Yes. The sadness overwhelms me. The parades and sacrificial celebrations are both a distraction and a reward for the hardship in their lives, temporary relief of the plenitude of sorrow that assails them.

This is the great test of mankind; the test of righteousness of being. To act in goodness and grace in a land of greed, spite, and materialism is no easy feat whilst surrounded by a sea of violence, hate, and betrayal. Drowning in their own selfishness and egotism, they ask, what's in it for me?

The test of mankind is the seen versus the unseen, the physical versus the spiritual. The flesh left wanting or the Spirit left wanting? They fail to understand it is a double-edged sword, for sure. Greed, theft, rape, murder - their choices are with them for eternity, like a shroud of grief around a shame they cannot name. It is the shame of their Soul's neglect, the rejection of their divinity, and the wasted choices of their life.

To live in righteousness of being with no immediate Earthly reward in such a materialistic world is a mighty test of being human. It is the test of aligning to the will of God. The test of faith. Many blessings are upon those who live a righteous life. Giving always benefits the giver more so than the receiver.

But how can I judge? I feel that I, too, have a collection of wasted choices in my repertoire of sins. I could have done more. In my earlier prime, petty squabbles and trivialities side-tracked me from the true purpose of life. Such power plays! Whose memories or interpretations were correct? Whose version of the Gospel took precedence? Such were the unbecoming melodramas of the church. Adjustments were made here and there, early on, to make the Word more palatable for the less enlightened. This was indeed a travesty of the highest. I could have protested more strongly, but now that horse has bolted. God grant me mercy on my Soul.

The long years of retrospection enable such clarity in old age. And what have I become? Do I truly know myself? I am proud of the work I have done for God, spreading wisdom to the masses. And yet, I feel I should have done more, I should be *doing* more. I have become complacent, I sigh, and I ponder the ramifications of this.

Is it I to blame for the increased pagan worship all around? Is the influence of the church diminished now? What more can I do to stop this barbarity? The worship of false gods had started to wane in years gone by, but now has taken on a new lease of life. Some of the city elders support the activities, especially the craftsmen and traders; increased trade is not something they would lightly turn their backs on. Profits before prophets, no less. I chuckle to myself. I lay my weary head down to rest. Just a short nap and then I will resume my tasks. No rest for the dutiful among us!

Do not burden yourself with guilt, for the guilty
know that life is a tapestry, and the threads do

join and pull apart and repairs are many. It is
the quality of the seamstress and the dedication
to the whole – the whole of life, the full picture,
the choice of threads, the colour in the making
– that ensures your tapestry is bright and woven
with love and wisdom of the Highest. Do not seek
to pull apart the scenes which trouble you now.
Repair all holes, all loose threads, and the work
will be seamless, the beauty sustained, and the
damage contained. This is progress, this is life,
and you will be astounded. The journey of your
life is a tapestry of light woven silk and golden
rays of love; such quality of the highest.

I awake with the birdsong and realise I have slept the whole night through. Very unusual for my bladder. I awake with a renewed vigour and purpose. I will challenge the status quo. I will challenge the traders, money lenders, barkeeps, and craftsmen about their unwavering support of paganism in their midst. I will not turn a blind eye, as in the past, in order to keep the peace. For what use knowledge if not shared with the world?

What would Jesus do? Would he sit by, silent and idle, or assist them with wisdom and loving grace to find their true path? I ask for inspiration from the Highest. The pagan gods are powerful, in so much as they hold the populace in thrall of dire punishments if their rules are not followed to the letter. But these are man-made rules, no less. Such fear and terror they incite. They are indeed considered jealous and petty gods, demanding all, and arbitrarily dispensing favours and protection at will. This is what their followers believe; such randomness befounds them.

I understand, naturally, the need for people to blame someone or something for any misfortune or luck in their lives. However, the gods they worship are not to blame. They are not gods, per se. They are simply Spirits, as we, too, are Spirits – we are Spirits currently living a physical existence on Earth. They are powerful Spirit entities, yes, but they are not gods, and they are not jealous and petty. They are Master Spirits, and they help mankind in many ways, just as there are many Spirit Guides who help mankind evolve. They are benign Spirits. They do not cause untold misery and destruction if they are not appeased, that is simply superstition.

God gave us all free will so that we can choose our own destiny. We create the conditions of our life by the righteous choices that we make. Yet, people often feel they do not have free will over their lives. They think that events that unfold are completely beyond their control, orchestrated by some invisible architect of destruction. They prefer to attribute failures and hardships to someone more potent, as they themselves feel impotent when faced with the tests of life.

Traders and craftsmen – especially the woodcarvers, the stonemasons, and the silversmiths – encourage the worship of deities and the rituals of sacrifice, all done at the feet of their likenesses in the form of statues and effigies. The degree of devotion by these traders and craftsmen to these rites and rituals is only surpassed by the constant flow of wealth these activities deliver them.

I chuckle and then sigh. I cannot believe people are so gullible. What little silver they have saved they spend on the altar of sacrifice, while their children go hungry and unshod. What travesty is this? Artemis, the overseer of infants, would be aghast at this neglect. She is a loving Master Spirit who, as protector of mothers and unborn infants, would never countenance such cruelty and neglect in her name. Such a twisted variation on her tradition. How did it come to this?

There is only one true God and he is loving and wise. The test of life is to have faith *despite* what misfortune becomes us, not seek to blame God and jealously despise those deemed more fortunate. We all have tests in life, big and small, and the universe is perfectly balanced. This may not be apparent from the viewpoint of this singular lifetime, but all is known, all is balanced in the Record Book of Life, of *all* our many lives. Materialism, wealth, and power are not the Soul's criteria for measuring success in this world.

We cannot see another's Soul journey, so we cannot judge another based on their fortune or misfortune in this life alone. We must worry about our own Soul journey, pure and simple, not covet our neighbour's good fortune when we know not where they have been and the depths their Soul may have journeyed before awakening to the light of God. We know nothing of their lessons undertaken over many lives, in this school of life on Earth. Nor do we know what pain and sorrow is carried deep in their baggage of surrender.

We must not envy, we must not hate, and we must not judge. We must instead honour each Soul journey. And we must never blame another or blame God for our choices in life or our absence of faith, for God created us with free will.

We are not puppets; there is no puppet-master to blame for the choices that we make, or the way we live our lives.

Righteousness is a choice that will make your
heart sing. Glory to the choir of the true believers,
as the Choir Master sings along and the tuneful
play their part in the opera of their lives.

Unification of Spirit and Soul, that is what our being craves. Our Soul is the repository of all the wisdom we acquire over many lifetimes. All the life lessons, the successes, and the failures, provide great knowledge for the Soul. Focus on the journey of your Soul, the eternal journey. Look to the future and make choices you are proud of.

Do not pin your hopes of a better life on those deities you consider gods, those idols you worship. They are not wicked and blood-thirsty gods, seeking revenge and out to smite those who fail to observe the many sacrificial rites that mankind has devised. Why does mankind insist on following increasingly elaborate superstitions, dogma, and rituals verging on witchcraft, to show their true devotion to these pagan gods of old?

Thanks be to God that our humble church is not overcome by such dogma, rituals, power, and pretence. It is based on simplicity of the Word. I pray to God that it never gets corrupted by those who seek to simultaneously intimidate and mollify the masses in order to keep them in their place. That would be such a travesty and complete anathema of what Jesus stands for.

Simplicity of life is the message Jesus came to share. A

simple life of unconditional love; love of God, love of oneself, and love of each other. Simple kindness and compassion – that is love in action! Not sacrificial beasts of burden on the altar of prosperity. Not ritual violence and orgies under cover of drunken festivities. Not favours for some, but no bread to share. No, our church is pure and righteous, and the Word of God has set us free. I pray to God that our teachings remain pure and free from further contamination. It is such a responsibility to pass on before I have departed this Earth.

I stoop with the weight of responsibility upon me. Choosing my successor is a heavy burden. I feel weary and cold, and I reach for some mulled wine to warm my bones. My cat cannot resist a taste. He coils around my feet and purrs with impatient gratitude. He is the luckiest cat in town, I truly do believe. So safe, so secure, with no worries in this world. A simple life of devotion and dedication; no complications, no toadying to those in power, just genuine affection for all he meets. An ideal road map for us all, I suppose.

It is a reciprocal arrangement, no doubt. In my mind, his companionship and affection represent adequate repayment for his meagre rations. His mousing days are long behind him, despite his hunting skills being the sole factor in securing his tenure with my housekeeper in the first place. It would appear his years of easy retirement will stretch out much further than his preceding years of gainful productivity. What use a cat, if not a mouse can catch? I chuckle to myself….. What use a Bishop, if not a Soul can save?

I ponder some more on the issue of corruption of the Word. Already, some influential debaters have sought to change the church's teachings. Of course, Jesus was clear in his wisdom

– all are equal in this world and the next. God has created us thus. And yet... and yet...*still* they seek to diminish the role of women. Still they seek to elevate those with wealth and power to a more pious status. Subtly, oh so subtly, they seek to influence how the Word is transcribed. Even the sermons to the masses do not escape scrutiny and are criticised if not considered in their best interests. Such vanity!

The wealthy benefactors are easily displeased, and the coffers would be empty without their patronage. Not *all* the wealthy, of course, just the greedy and vainglorious. There are enough to cause my stomach to churn. Oh, how it gives me such discomfort. They seek to control everything in their world, that is their wont. If only they knew that their Souls are crying out to be set free from all that holds them back. All the materialistic greed, the power-plays that seek to judge people as lesser than their own good selves, the selfishness, the envy, the bigotry and hate, the ignorance, and the apathy to the needs of others – these are all obstacles in the way of their progression to the light.

If they truly understood the teachings that Jesus came to share, they would understand that their need to control the world is simply due to fear. Greed is those who take regardless of their need. Greed is the mind's response to fear. Fear is the opposite of love, and fear withers their Soul.

Fear will get them nowhere fast. It will harden as a heavy weight upon their heart and all will see the agony that resides there. When you understand that material wealth is worthless in the land of your Soul, such freedom abounds! This is the truth that will set mankind free; free from fear of betrayal and loss, free from obsessing about your next acquisition, free from envy of others more overburdened than yourself.

The only treasure you truly need in this life is in the treasure chest of your heart; such treasure to share with all you meet. Like leavened bread to share around, you rise and shine the light of God and share the goodness of your Soul. Kindness, compassion, and truth to all – what gifts to leave the world! What gifts to be inscribed on the Record Book of Life for all eternity.

> *Every day in every way the Light is there to guide*
> *us. It ushers in a new day dawning and all will*
> *see the Light that is beholden to the Lord.*
> *The world evolves, and the evolution of*
> *mankind is a joy to behold.*

I turn to the Holy Chalice as tears fill my eyes. What would Jesus say? What would Jesus do? He was always so forthright with the rich and powerful. His passion was for all mankind, but he certainly had a special affinity with the sick, the poor, and the outcasts among us. The cripples, the beggars, the thieves – he understood their pain of life, the burdens on their Soul. He could see their Soul's journey thus far, and the baggage they did carry. He soothed, he healed, and he loved them unconditionally. Real love – not just for show, not for the audience gathering in the square, but real tenderness and care. They could see it in his eyes, his light emanated all around, and all could feel his love. Like honey in the air, it was golden light for all to share. Many miracles became him, and the light of God enveloped all who came to bask in the aura of his being – the Christ Light, the sacred divine light of

God. Jesus was the lantern bearer of light who came to save the world with his holy flame.

We beseech you dear Lord, please return to save our Souls once more from the pain and suffering of life. Many do not understand the pain they bear, and the residue of lives lived in sorrow. Many are pining but know not what they lack. They are fed and yet they hunger. They drink and yet they thirst. They wake and yet they sleepwalk. They live a human, inter-connected life and yet they wither in neglect of their hearts and each other.

Reckless is the heart when the mind is in charge.
Reckless is the pain of yesteryear when it closes
in and fills your heart with sorrow. To look at
the future with love in your heart and wisdom
in your Soul, and to ride the wave of destiny, is a
journey of the brave, the loyal, and the faithful.

Chapter 5

The ending is the beginning.

❖

Today is an important pagan festival and there is excitement in the air. There are many festivities to be had, including a parade. The stall holders in the market square, and along the temple road, are busier than ever selling effigies of the goddess Artemis, as well as silver trinkets.

Date, figs, honey, and sweetmeats are the feast offerings of choice, and many will see their tables laden with the food of the gods. I wonder how many of my dear brethren will make their way to the square to join with the revellers later this day. I may indeed go for a walk myself to see the action unfold. I do take pleasure in seeing the children enjoying themselves.

The poor and the hungry often get more food than they are used to this day, as the discarded sacrificial meat is distributed to the crowds. All types of foods may be dropped or cast aside by the drunken revellers, and the children in need are always underfoot, ready to pounce at the first opportunity. It is comforting to see that some good, at least, arises from these idolatrous spectacles.

Nonetheless, I wrestle with the nagging feeling that I must do more to stop this superstitious nonsense and bring more people into the embrace of the church. Have I been too complacent?

I re-read the words provided to me in the night from the realms of the Holy Spirit. The wonderful words of inspiration really do enliven my old heart and keep me well and truly motivated on my journey through this life.... or at least, what little time is left of it now, I chuckle.

> *Many are the times we called your name. Many*
> *are the fruits of your endeavours. Betwixt*
> *the Angels and the Guides, you are loved and*
> *cherished. You understand the trust we have*
> *in you. You fulfill the tasks and are not found*
> *wanting. The way to hope and glory is to come*
> *inside the future of your mind. The pain of the*
> *lost hope of redemption will ease. The Love and*
> *Light will summon all that soothes your heart of*
> *gold. Beware the journey of doubt. It eats away*
> *at all that is rich and fulfilling.*

I recall that on this feast day, more so than the others, the magicians work very hard to convince their audience that they have the favour of the gods onside, especially the ever-popular goddess Artemis. The magic tricks aim to demonstrate that they have a direct link to the wonders of the Heavens, a special connection they can exploit at will. I sigh, knowing full well that I round the bend of hypocrisy now, understanding that I, too, peddle in direct connections to God and the divine spiritual realms. The difference being, of course, that God – the one true God – is an all-knowing, all-loving, all-forgiving God who cannot be tricked, deceived, or coerced into bestowing his favourable attentions.

These magicians seek to buy favour and good fortune from Artemis with their sacrifices, magic, and baubles, no less. Naturally, this magical influence is predictably conditional on receipt of sufficient donations from the crowd. Their deceptions fall apart at the merest scrutiny. It is all about profit, pure and simple. Better tricks, bigger crowds, more silver!

Big crowds attract even bigger crowds, as people do not want to miss the magic of the day. Supposing the gods notice their absence? They believe that perhaps the gods will smile on them, too, if they show their true devotion. A bet each way will cover their anxieties. If only they would stake a claim on the internal wisdom of their heart and their direct connection to their Soul, they would be relieved of the burden of placing their trust (and their silver) in tricksters and frauds.

Anyone with a modicum of intelligence and wit can surely see the trickery? The problem is that they don't want to. They want to believe that these pagan gods rule their lives, finding favour and fault, bestowing riches and good fortune at will. A sacrifice here, a ritual there, a bonfire to their vanities; how much is enough?

Jesus understood the need of the people to put their faith in something bigger than themselves, to gain hope that the misery in their lives would not prevail. They hoped that the harvest would not be blighted, nor the livestock stolen. They hoped their children would not starve, the house would not burn down, and the invaders would not kill or maim them in the streets. So many worries, too many to name, and the hope spread thin.

Jesus understood their fears, and their mindsets. He loved them so. He sought to provide understanding of their eternal Souls and thus, the true meaning of their lives and their struggles. He provided hope and taught of the grace and simplicity of a life lived with humility and faith.

> *Faith is unwavering, unstoppable, a mighty flame of resistance to the ills of life. Faith is a milestone to be reached, a shore to be sighted, a horizon to be gazed at. Faith is the hunger of the Soul to rise above the daily grind that is life on Earth and reach to greater heights.*

The gatherings of Jesus were often simple affairs, not elaborate shows of power and might. His spiritual healing miracles were not proffered as magic to convince them that God was on his side. Many times, few people were even there to witness such events taking place. These miracles were not magic but were blessings from God, blessings of the highest.

Such a small word 'faith,' but such mighty power. The power to know with all of your being that God has a plan for you, for your life, and that you are loved and precious. Your journey is long and arduous, but you are a true believer in the power of Spirit, and the power of faith. You see the glory of the divine Christ Light and understand the true purpose of your life on Earth, relishing the chance to do good deeds and live your life the best you can. Such peace and harmony for your Soul.

We seek to continue the tradition of Jesus in the way we run the church. Simple events carried out several times per week; simple services of devotion, gratitude, and wisdom. No magic, sacrifices, or costumes are required. This is exactly what Jesus wanted. Grand shows of power or displays of wealth do not signify who he was.

He would not have wanted a crucifix to represent him, as some are favouring. That much is also clear to me. That is not what he stands for. His Ministry is one of love and light, with compassion and kindness his guiding principles – feeding the poor, lifting the downtrodden, and healing the sick. And above all, he stood for *Peace on Earth*. The persecution, torture, blame, fear, and ignorance he faced are not the stand-out memories of his life that he would seek to remind us of daily in the iconography of the church.

> *When peace is upon the world, the dutiful can*
> *take their place on the Honour Board of Life, for*
> *peace is the elixir that sets love free.*

I chat to my housekeeper about the events of the day. Yes, she has been to the market already, she informs me, and the momentum of the city is gaining pace. The traders are overjoyed. So many visitors from surrounding lands have descended on the city and the town is swarming with donkeys, carts, soldiers, and country folk.

I retire to my room and pray. The urge to thank God for my life overcomes me. I thank God for my time with Jesus, in particular. My role as Scribe and teacher of the Word, continuing the Ministry of Jesus, has been the mission of my life. It is my joy, my reason for being, my Soul's purpose in this life. I serve God, and by serving God I serve my own Spirit, and progress my Soul with wisdom and grace. The truth of my existence has set me free, and I am a dutiful, loving servant of Christ.

I understand the tests of life, the trials and tribulations that test our faith and test the very mettle of our being. Our moral fibre must withstand such tests. But do not despair if we fail a test, as God forgives us always. And so, we should forgive ourselves, for it is not God who will judge us when we enter the Kingdom of Heaven and review our thoughts, words and actions as recorded in the Record Book of our Life. We are our own judge and jury. The Angels applaud our efforts, and thus we begin again on the Wheel of Life. Another day, another life, another chance to make the right choices and progress our Soul's journey with love in our hearts and wisdom to share. And all around the Spirits do declare:

Believe in love, and all your burdens dissolve to dust. Have faith and you will prosper. The day has come to lay your baggage down. Start afresh, start anew, and usher in a new day for your Soul; a new beginning to surrender to the light of God. Redemption is the fruit of life, redeem yourself and your life will be bounteous.

I sit at my desk and begin to write. My heart is heavy with a pain I cannot name. I feel leaden and slow, my bones more stiffened than usual. What is this pain that grips me? Is it fear, I wonder? I know the answer and my resolve hardens. I plan to confront the pagan worshippers this day. I will no longer ignore the drunken debauchery right on the doorstep of this sacred place, this holy church.

The violence, the drunkenness – all in honour of Artemis, who truth be known would be ashamed of all the depravity and orgiastic worship undertaken in her name. No different than if Mary, mother of Jesus, were exalted in such a fashion. It is such an abomination of all that is good and true of the divine feminine light. I feel so sad that it has come to this.

My writing commences with a slow and steady hand. What message is of importance this day?

> *Be courageous in your stance. Do not turn a*
> *blind eye to what you know is wrong. Be wise,*
> *for your years reveal your wisdom, and a steady*
> *heart and steady gaze will see you to the door.*
> *Forget the voice of doubt. Be humble as you*
> *deliver the Word of God. This is your birthright,*
> *and the Angels will assist as you tread carefully*
> *down the path of good intentions. Forever know*
> *that you are loved, and you are worthy, and*
> *we bow to your true endeavours of the Soul.*
> *A joyous ride, a Chariot no less, will take you*
> *to your home. Go now, as the Angels sing your*
> *praises. All is known, all is as it should be. And*
> *Heaven knows your name, hallelujah.*

Tears fill my eyes and pride fills my heart. I feel a yearning for home. Not my boyhood home – that is by now a far-off memory like a fevered dream. Rather, it is a yearning for a spiritual home, one I know I have seen but cannot recall in detail. The sense of belonging overwhelms me. The feeling it espouses in me is a comforting, all-embracing wash of love and light, like a gentle sunlight on the heart. I take a moment to bask in this ray of pure, spiritual ecstasy and give thanks again to God the Almighty, Creator of Heaven and Earth.

My heart is ablaze with love and gratitude for this spiritual connection to the divine light of God. I am truly blessed to know such things are possible. When you have faith, all things are possible, that much I know. And my faith is strong, and strong, too, is my love for all mankind. I must tell them what I know. I must make them aware of God's love for them, and the wisdom Jesus came to share. I must heal them of their spiritual pain, their emptiness. This will bring them such peace. Mankind is crying out for peace in their heart, for they are truly suffering. And the pain is so raw, so palpable.

If only they understood the truth of life – that we are part of God and he is part of us, and that we are all interconnected. If only they knew that their choices in life are with them for all eternity, the choices that create baggage on their Souls. Such a weighty burden to carry through eternity. Heavy baggage that they accumulate with each life they live unless they rectify with love – unconditional love and forgiveness to all who wrong them.

My message is simple. All they need for a joyful life is love. They must turn away from greed, hate, and violence. War, rape, and pillage are mankind's downfall, the last echoes of thunder in the nightscape of their immorality.

THE ENDING IS THE BEGINNING.

*Holy are the believers of the Lord who lead where
they would follow, who lay their burdens down
and succumb to the divine light, the Christ
Light that leads us home. This is the heart-song
for all to learn; memorise the lines and hum
the tune to eternity.*

Reflecting the love and light and higher vibration of God represents righteousness of being, and this will bring enlightenment, a reunification of the Soul with *all that is* – the closer to God the Father. Heaven and Earth are filled with his glory!

People are pining to understand their purpose in life, and this knowledge will bring such joy. The knowing is in the living and the living is in the knowing. No longer wandering in the wilderness, they will climb the pinnacle of their Soul and understand that the truth they sought was there all along. In the recesses of their heart they find the key to happiness, the wisdom to set them free from the tyranny of life. The truth of their being.

*Harness the truth to save the day, harness the
light above. Bathe in light, love, and hope, for the
future of mankind. For when you seek the light,
become the light, your future is revealed; the
future that is bright, the future that is round the
bend. Love will have its day and love will show
the way. Love is.*

—

The sun is high in the sky by the time I stir from my reverie. My writing has been abundant this day. I organise my parchments and retreat to the small kitchen, an outhouse behind the church. I have a taste for honeycomb, and I raid the larder that is usually locked. My housekeeper is not too far away, tending the kitchen garden. The birds are singing the praises of the Lord, I note, such beauty in the birdsong.

I return to my room with a morsel of meat for my cat. I stroke his fur. No words are necessary. He understands me, and I, him. He knows I love and appreciate him. The pure love of an animal is hard to replicate, except in children, of course. Theirs is unconditional love, innocence, and joyful endeavours of the heart. The best of life; the best of mankind. Jesus reminded us that we should all be as pure of heart as little children, so as to enter the Kingdom of Heaven with ease.

There is beauty and splendour in a heart opened to all. A heart of grey that is closed off, shuttered, heavy, or dull, serves no-one fast. It must be a rainbow of light, a kaleidoscope of golden love for all to share. Your heart is your connection to the divine light of Heaven. It is the seat of purpose, the vault of memory, the key to all you need to travel in this life upon the pathway of your Soul.

Take care of your heart, feed it daily with kindness and good deeds to all, and you will not be found wanting. For a heart that is open is a heart that sings the song of praises to our Lord. A heart that fills the room with tenderness and care, is a heart so big it cannot be contained in the human vessel. It reaches out to all with compassion and grace and understands that the heart knows what the head may not – that love is the elixir of life.

THE ENDING IS THE BEGINNING.

A heart for all seasons is a heart to be proud of.

A heart starved of love is pitiful indeed. It must give love to receive love. Unrequited love, if given freely with no expectation of return, is never a burden on the Soul. It finds its mark and the universe responds. Unconditional love is the test of mankind and many fail this test time and time again. It takes courage and bravery to fully open your heart to all. The heart is no stranger to despair and longing, and you will find that an active heart is a heart that knows the story of the Soul.

I leave my beloved church, a simple house structure but so noble in its presence. I make my way to the main square, and I greet the revellers grouped on each corner as I round my way past them. There is music and dancing, feasting, and drinking. Many hawkers and magicians are spruiking their wares. Costumes are plentiful; masks enabling many to loosen their inhibitions along with their pockets. The prostitutes are roaming, emboldened by the crowds of drinkers and the silver freely changing hands. Petty arguments can be heard above the din. Violent fisticuffs, knives unsheathed, children being spat and cursed at – what mayhem is this?

I walk the streets, seeing no-one I recognise at first glance. The horror show appears to be just beginning. Perhaps I am just too old, and less tolerant of the times, I surmise. After all, I, too, love wine. It is the perfect antidote to a nervous stomach. It helps keep away the winter chill, relaxing the bones and the mind, enabling a restful sleep.

I try to relax and be tolerant of those who cross my path, but it appears that rudeness is the order of the day. The drunken pushing, shoving, cursing, spitting and more, is a degrading spectacle. Have they no respect for themselves or each other? I pass a loveless couple fornicating in a doorway and I drive away the gawking children. Such hedonistic behaviour. Oh, the baseness and banality of life, why are we tested so?

I walk the length of the trading stalls to see what is on offer. Nothing new, just the usual effigies and trinkets. The smell of the food is enticing. Honey cakes and sweetbreads, whole roasted meats, nuts, bread, and olives. The children play, excited that their usual routine is interrupted. I see one grab a fig that has fallen off a cart onto the ground. She runs away laughing, her friends in hot pursuit. The air is dusty and still, the bonfire smoke settling low. No-one appears to notice my existence, not even the traders, and I feel largely invisible to the crowds.

As I walk slowly, I am aware of divine communication. I do not question this, as I have learnt over many years to always expect the unexpected. I am slightly taken aback at the timing, but I endeavour to remember it for later when I return to the church:

The Changing of the Guard

The fortunes of the brave, the wisdom of the Age.
The starlight of your Soul,
the love to make you whole.
A glorious endeavour indeed.
Jesus comes to those who call his name.

THE ENDING IS THE BEGINNING.

His love is infinite.
His light, the healing touch of God.

Many a time he said to thee:
Stand tall and you will know no doubt,
Your heart is open, loving, and wise.
With grace you see your duty done.
The Chariot awaits your Holy Spirit, awash with
the righteousness of thee.

Beautiful words, I do concede, but I delay my opportunity to fully digest their meaning. I walk with more urgency now towards the temple where a huge crowd is milling around. This is it, I sigh, summoning courage deep within me. I must be brave. I must be righteous. I must say something now or forever hold my peace. I can no longer turn a blind eye to what is happening in this city and still claim to serve the Lord.

What would Jesus do? He would find the right words to get his point across with wisdom and grace. He always did so with an open heart of such beauty and grandeur. Jesus, please give me the strength and the wisdom to do what I must do. I must correct this abomination that is occurring under my watch. I must convince the people that there is only one true God. These gods they worship are false idols. They should choose instead to follow God's will and live in righteousness and truth, just as you have taught us.

Let God's will be their will! Joyful serenity will be their fortune if they choose to live another way. The light of God will be upon them; the Holiest of the Holy, Maker of Heaven and Earth. Deliver us Lord from all that pains us, deliver us to the light. For we are free, and duty bound to serve our one true love.

*You carry the Word within your heart and
none so sure of God's true Word than those who
look into the eyes of love and understand the
glory of the task – the glory that is theirs to
share, the love of all humanity, and the truth
to set them free.*

I walk amongst the throng of people jostling at the temple entrance. Someone has roasted a goat, I notice, and the smoke from the sacrificial beast is sweet upon the air. I see a large, empty pot and turn it upside down. I step up and get a better view of my surroundings. I am unsteady on my feet, but my resolve is unwavering. This, I must do.

The words seem to come out of nowhere. I start talking and the words flow rather eloquently – if I do say so myself.

"My dear brothers and sisters of this fine city..." Heads turn, and I have their attention. Their curiosity is evident. *"I implore you all to cease your idolatrous ways. This is not the way of God, your one true God, the Creator of all that is. This is barbarity, an offence to God! There is only one God. I implore you to put aside these pagan practices of old. They have no place here….."*

Before I can finish, a loud jeer goes up from a man in the crowd and I am pelted with a pomegranate. It splits in two upon contact with the side of my head, and I feel faint, but mostly I am shocked at the impudence of the act. I continue on with my pleas, but the crowd is now aroused. No-one is listening to me, their jeers drowning out my impassioned pleas for abstinence from their ungodly rituals.

I feel saddened. A part of me already knows what the future holds, and I feel I am not ready.

> *The dewdrops know that theirs is a fall of grace*
> *and harmony, a divine task of love that sees*
> *their duty done.*

A masked man steps forward, clearly inebriated. He raises his tankard as if to toast me then throws the contents in my face. As the tankard is emptied, he spits on me and shouts that I am an old fool who should mind his own business. I glance around the crowd for some semblance of support and I notice one or two familiar faces who step away when they see the focus of my gaze. They move out of view behind others who are now all forming a circle around what has clearly become the biggest spectacle of the day so far.

My voice is wavering slightly, but I continue with my protest, despite the jeering that has erupted. I remind them of God's love for all of mankind, and the truth that Jesus came to share. "*It is not too late to redeem yourself; it is never too late to turn your back on idolatry and turn to the love and light of God the Father, the Creator of all that is.*"

There is a sense of blood lust in the air. The drunken crowd, in freewheeling frenzy, is clearly looking for an outlet to expend their excess energy. At this point a blow is rained upon my shoulder from a heavy rock, and I fall heavily to the ground. In breathless agony, I feel a searing pain in my ribs. Frenzied kicking and stomping on my head and body begins in earnest. I am disoriented. *Where is the church?* I wonder. *Perhaps I can make it back somehow. I'll be safe there.....*

Tears fill my eyes as the pain rips through my body. Was it worth it?

Before the blackness overcomes me, my final thoughts are of Jesus. *Dear Jesus, I love you like a brother. You are everything to me. Please forgive me.*

I become aware of a Choir of Angels singing. Oh, the bliss!

"*Come, my dear one*", Jesus replies, as the Angels alight the Chariot.

"*All is forgiven. It is time to take you home.*"

THE ENDING IS THE BEGINNING.

Life as we know it is a battle laid to waste.
A new life begins forthwith.
A life of simplicity, love, and compassion for all.
The planet reels, the dust settles, and all are
home to roost.
The magnanimity of hate and spite and loveless
existence is understood at last.
Greed is empty, hate is bare, and sorrow takes
our breath away.

Epilogue

Dear Reader....

❖

Cherish this time. The future is assured, and you will see that all will understand the future as it unfolds; the future of mankind in the stand, farewelling greed, hypocrisy, hate, and war.

What will it take to understand that the ways of the world are changing? The classroom heaves, the scholars retreat, and all is as it should be. Lessons are learnt, life goes on, and hate and fear subside.

It behoves us now to take a stand for all that is righteous and true. Reject the fear, the hate, the greed. Understand the truth that lays there waiting, ready to take your hand.

Wallow in the ecstasy of love, and light, and the true surrender to the divine. For this is the time to let your Spirit soar. This is the time to reach to the clouds and let no-one drag you down.

The mountaintop beckons, the stars align, and destiny's doorstep awaits the final countdown. All power to those who know that majesty becomes them.

DEAR READER....

These are the footsteps of love. Follow them now and you will be astounded as your dreams are answered, and the Holy gather to see what you are made of.

The light glows forth, the heart is open, and love reigns supreme. Listen to your heart, it knows the way. And the light will shine forever more, hallelujah.

A Message to the Faithful

Talk to thee, walk with thee, and I shall lead you home.
Never again shall the glory evade you, for you are blessed to know full glory of the Word.
We salute you, old friend.
The summer sun is set to shine, and all will be revealed.
You are lost no more.